M

NIGHT BATTLE

Also by WILLIAM LOGAN

POETRY

Sad-faced Men (1982)
Difficulty (1985)
Sullen Weedy Lakes (1988)
Vain Empires (1998)

CRITICISM

All the Rage (1998)
Reputations of the Tongue (1999)

PENGUIN BOOKS
Published by the Penguin Group
Penguin Putnam Inc., 375 Hudson Street,
New York, New York 10014, U.S.A.
Penguin Books Ltd, 27 Wrights Lane,
London W8 5TZ, England
Penguin Books Australia Ltd, Ringwood,
Victoria, Australia
Penguin Books Canada Ltd, 10 Alcorn Avenue,
Toronto, Ontario, Canada M4V 3B2
Penguin Books (N.Z.) Ltd, 182–190 Wairau Road,
Auckland 10, New Zealand

Penguin Books Ltd, Registered Offices:
Harmondsworth, Middlesex, England

First published in Penguin Books 1999

1   3   5   7   9   10   8   6   4   2

LIBRARY OF CONGRESS CATALOGING IN PUBLICATION DATA
Logan, William, 1950–
    Night battle: poems/by William Logan.
        p.   cm. — (Penguin poets)
    ISBN 0 14 05.8798 5
    I. Title.
    PS3562.O449N54   1999
    811'.54—dc21   99–19548

Printed in the United States of America
Set in Fairfield
Designed by Mia Risberg

NIGHT BATTLE

Poems by

✣ WILLIAM LOGAN ✣

 PENGUIN POETS

for George and Zara Steiner

Contents

ACKNOWLEDGMENTS

Agni: Seductions of the Swimming Club; *American Literary Review:* The Cities of the Plain; Kant; The Words; *Antioch Review:* Gray's Anatomy; *Arion:* Beauty; *Columbia:* Border Sonnets v ("Thunderstorm"); Border Sonnets vi ("Slugs"); *Gettysburg Review:* Song; *Gulf Coast:* Luxury; *Hudson Review:* Nativity; *Iowa Review:* Living; *Metropolitan Review:* The English Light; *The Nation:* Border Sonnets iv ("Vesuvius"); The Late Perpendicular of England; The Livery of Byzantium; *New Criterion:* After a Line by F. Scott Fitzgerald; Blues for Penelope; Elegy; *New England Review:* My Father as Madame Butterfly; *The New Yorker:* Border Sonnets i ("Iowa"); Dear DD; Nothing; *Notre Dame Review:* St. John and the Wasps; *Paris Review:* Bad Dream; Border Sonnets iii ("Insects"); Eden in the Dustbowl; Mother on the St. Johns; Sundays in the South; *Partisan Review:* For a Woman in United Germany; *Poetry:* Dear HM; For the Hostages; Larkin; *Prism International:* Adam and Eve; Auden at C——— C———; The Woods at M———; *Salmagundi:* Manhattan Transfers; *Sewanee Review:* Border Sonnets ii ("Water"); Border Sonnets vii ("The Dead Raccoon"); Leavis Before Christ's; Reading the Greek Gospels; *Southwest Review:* Dune House; Florida in January; The Old College; Small Bad Town; *The Times Literary Supplement:* Dear AC; *Verse:* Marx; Paradise; *Western Humanities Review:* The Lesser Depths; *Yale Review:* On the Crucifixions; The Shock of the New

"A Pilgrim of Pilgrims" appeared in *Articulations* (University of Iowa Press, 1994); "Niobe" in *After Ovid,* eds. James Lasdun and Michael Hofmann (Farrar, Straus & Giroux, 1995).

Harp? Harp? Lyre? Pen and ink, boy,
you mean! Muse, boy, Muse? Your
nurse's daughter, you mean! Pierian
spring? Oh 'aye! the cloister-pump, I
suppose!

Biographia Literaria

NIGHT BATTLE

The American Scene

Florida in January

The cold of winter is somehow colder here,
the trees bleaker, with their rags of Spanish moss,
the very air clipped and impatient.
You wouldn't realize summer's forest,
so much like New England, grew in a mattress of marsh,
until the leaves were down. Beneath the second growth
a low fringe of starved palmettos
lives in short, childlike arcs, their palest greens
worn almost to the color of old dollar bills.
In rye fields and feed lots,
amid the swaying, wheezing cattle
lost to their mute philosophies,
stalk our self-important tourists, the sandhill cranes—
Nature's aristocrats, eyes flared with red eye-shadow
(carelessly applied, as if without a mirror),
their jaunty icepick heads eager or greedy,
but their bodies delicately boned, like young ballerinas.
They high-step away in virginal unease.

Nothing repairs the indifference of their veering,
neither the storm casting its tattered cloak
over the sand pines, nor egrets huddled
against the lake's border, folded up like origami paper,
nor the water, sullen, pocked and greasy,
a rusting tintype of our latent democratic vistas.
Like Ovid on the Black Sea, the restless stranger
might feel such cruel beauty monotonous.
But, inshore, a crusty alligator steams,
nosing into reeds to let off passengers
or take on canvas sacks of mail,
as if the weather had never once been tender
or required, like love, a moment of surrender.

Sundays in the South

The gravid gecko lies
aslant a stalk of banana,
just a tilde over
the *n* in *mañana*,

translucent as a thin
slice of kiwi fruit,
with two small beads—
or seeds!—for eyes. The root

of all evil is motion,
its body seems to say.
A crab spider looks it over
as it overlooks prey.

With a ticking, pebbly rattle,
tubercular pigeons sun
on the hot tin roof,
the roof of Sin,

burning, burning
over those fierce Christians
sinning—or singing, perhaps,
much louder than sinning.

The pigeons roost in judgment,
mottled, maculate angels,
complacent but nervous
above the stacked cannonballs.

Heat is a form of love,
boasts the courthouse square
to the Frank Lloyd Wright
air conditioner.

Fruit bats lodged in the eaves
shadow the low gas fire
of sunset, whose bankrupt palms
open their broken armatures

like Edwardian ladies
at the season's last tea dance—
black fans, black fans!
And, at a distance,

thunder, a great steamroller,
rumbles now with a sad consent
over the tropics' grandeur
and diminishment.

Mother on the St. Johns

The palms looked wary in broad afternoon,
thin women in fancy ribbed hats.
Beyond them the hooded sweep of the St. Johns

gathered home the overweight mariners,
yachting caps askew as the afternoon broke up
and boats shuddered to the bank.

Indoors, beside your chaise longue, cigarettes
were burning mad, their heads alight.
You lit them one after another,

as if you could torture them all.
The condo's wide-screen TV blocked your view.
All life was now a miniseries,

and the Florida sky, that great brocaded curtain,
was about to be drawn over the closing night,
where a thorny, ungrateful gator

wallowed on the shared ledge of bank,
home, or willing to call it home,
the incoherent kingdom. And then a heron took off,

beating its wings like a broken angel,
neck crooked backward in a childlike Z.
Its arc hesitated above the palms.

Darker, but not so injured now.

LONG ISLAND SINS

i. Seductions of the Swimming Club

The working mothers never worked aloud,
those afternoons spent poolside, lean and tanned
amid the apparitions of the crowd.
The petals of their suits were caked with sand.
No black face ever troubled their repose.
At sunset servants in white uniforms
showered the greasy dust off with a hose
as summer broke the dark with lightning storms.
We drank in their politeness like a sin;
each deferential sir, each honeyed ma'am
reminded us that powers ranged above us.
Our mothers drank martinis and sweet gin:
we were too young for anyone to love us.
That fall our boys invaded Vietnam.

ii. A Pilgrim of Pilgrims

At 91, coldcocked on Demerol,
Grandmother basks among the hyacinths,
lost to the stale, sweet pall of Jacksonville,
the lazy river and its hoodlum boats.
My thin aunts squabble like young mockingbirds.
A skeleton among the skeletons,
no blood egg on your finger, the highboy sold,
your cheekbones crazed translucent as onionskin.
The doctors would give you up, have given you up,
your pittance of stock now all utilities
("Natural gas, my dear—what dividends!").
A Kool balancing unlit between your fingers,
the throaty voice of childhood—doomed, not doomed—
calls for the first scotch and next cigarette.

iii. After a Line by F. Scott Fitzgerald

Southampton, Hot Springs, and Tuxedo Park:
lost in the backwash of the Crash, the War,
the refugees of grace were washed ashore.
The girls who once were "miffed" or "truly vexed"
would soon acquire the morals of a shark,
waltzing the railroad barons round the floor,
their cold, triumphant necks a jewelry store.
And in the shadows the next drink, and the next.
Where does it go, the moment of desire?
Lost, rattling down the Special's corridor,
the distant vein of lights in semaphore;
lost, the champagne glasses tossed against the fire,
the bullet laid inside a lower drawer.
And there is love, cruel love, the last to bore.

St. John and the Wasps

The scrub was dry, dry as pitch.
The naked wasps lifted their bodies
through the heavy air, and as they landed
on the crumpled paper globe, they shivered.
The globe was brown and dry as wrapping paper.
They scoured it like an army of salesmen.

Where do we go when we die?
We're born in heaven, like the wasps.

We had come to expect the plagues.
Why shouldn't the rivers stink?
Why shouldn't the water change to blood?
In the wet season, why shouldn't our houses
fill with the scream of frogs? In the dry,
why shouldn't the dust boil with maggots?
We have suffered the hail. We are covered with flies.
Why should the evening be better than the morning?

Now the boy lay
beneath the rafters eaten up with termites,
where moths outwaited the daylight,
where the small things devoured larger things.

The stunted palms, as tall as a man, disappeared
along the hammock. Delicately, unsteadily upright,
they faded into the cloudy undergrowth.
The canvas chaise was spotted with rosettes of mildew.
The boy was discolored, too.
He watched the wasps come and go, go and come,
as if they had found order on their little globe.
It was not a large world, as worlds go.

NIOBE

The upland farmers are a breed apart,
tight with their money, closed-mouth, decent folk
who'd hay your lower pasture twice a year
if you caught sick, but wouldn't give a dime
to charity. They might just burn you out
if you argued with them over politics.
Up there you wouldn't sell your old John Deere
if you thought the axle was about to go.

I heard the story from a friend of mine,
who heard it from his brother's son-in-law
who heard it in a country-western bar.
Niobe was her name. She was no Yankee.
Her husband was a banker in New York—
he had a name in Wall Street arbitrage.
They'd bought a Berkshire farm for holidays
and used to stay through August. On Labor Day
they'd roar back to New York in BMW's.
It was the old Mackenzie place—you know it.
Played out for corn or pumpkin, but decent land
if you wanted just to sit and stare at it.
Kindling and boulder were its money crop.
She wore the latest fashions from Milan—
an Hermès handbag in the Stop & Shop
when people couldn't pay their mortgages.

Up-mountain lived a woman, the widow L.
The papers still refuse to print her name,
though afterward they knew just what had happened.
She had the twins, Apollo and Diana.
Even the nurses thought the names were strange,
but the twins were handsome, modest kids—
they stayed up on the farm and did their chores.
The widow L had a local reputation.

She hadn't been to town in twenty years,
but she was kind to some—sent down preserves,
a rhubarb pie if your husband was laid up.
She always sent a pie down for a funeral.
She wasn't a woman whom you dared to cross—
she had another sort of reputation.
No one hunted deer along that mountain.
They didn't take to strangers on the mountain.

Some other time, and nothing might have happened.
Some other place, and nothing would have happened.
Niobe never learned the country way—
she had a mouth, they say, looking for trouble.
Her mother's father was a *nouveau riche*,
her father a distinguished senator—
some folks had read about her in the *Bee*.
She had it all—a brownstone off Park Avenue,
a classic face that plastic surgery
could not improve, could not improve much further.
And she had seven sons and seven daughters.
She could have bought and sold that little town,
but she never understood how local folk
could talk about a woman they never saw,
and folks did talk about the mountain widow
as if she were a part-time village saint.
Perhaps it wasn't worship, not exactly,
not like the worship they managed in the church,
but it was, say, close cousin to such worship.
They liked her better for never having seen her.
Some said she'd been a teenage outcast, hounded
from town to town to have her bastard twins.
Some said that she'd been pregnant by her father.

Now townfolk never cottoned to Niobe.
You had to know her high heels were Italian,
her scarves were French, her rings were Tiffany's.
She was a walking advertisement for free trade.

She knew she had a lot to be grateful for,
but somehow she wanted you to be grateful too.
No wonder she was proud. How could fate touch her?
Even if God had taken a child or two,
she owned too much to know what losing was.
If the market crashed, her trusts were well protected;
she had the best investments money could buy,
the best of everything. But not the best of town.
Some people did amend their talk around her,
but she couldn't stop the whispering in private.

One morning in the bank she stood in line
behind two village gossips, who were deep
in some old story about the widow L.
Niobe crossed her arms and then let rip.
"Damned if I'll listen to another word
about this pig-eyed, ignorant mountain girl
who has two bastard twins and welfare checks.
If kids are what you farmers care about,
how many does she have? A measly two.
Just two. Why, I have seven times as many!
I'm fed up with that ghostly backwoods bitch
who had her little bastards out of wedlock
and bakes you rhubarb pie when you get buried."

No angry woman was more beautiful,
but there are things you never say aloud
about a stranger's mother. Word got around.
The twins had heard it. They knew what to do.
They dressed up in their hunter's camouflage,
though hunting season was a month away,
and took their bows down from the fireplace.
They took a sheaf of arrows barbed for deer . . .

The very youngest was the last to die,
down on his knees in Dr. Parker's hay field.
The only thing he said was "Please don't kill me."

For a moment, the twins regretted what they'd done,
but the final arrow was already away.
The local folks were stunned. There hadn't been
as many killed in the flood of '34.
The undertaker drove to Springfield for the coffins,
but no one said a word against the twins.
It was a justice understood up there.
You don't go looking at that sort of justice.
Some might have called it fate. It wasn't fate.
It wasn't more than what was right. And paid is paid.
Even her enemies had to pity her.
The Wall Street banker? Well, he cut his throat.
Folks thought the better of him after that.
The widow L sent down a rhubarb pie.

After the funerals, Niobe went insane.
The doctor said she turned as hard as stone.
Some say she really did turn into stone.
Some say her statue's on the mountaintop,
where acid rain erodes its granite face.
Some claim it weeps hot tears, like a wooden Virgin
in some church in Mexico. A miracle.

There *is* a woman's statue on the mountain.
I met some hikers once who said they'd seen it.

BLUES FOR PENELOPE

The roses are gone, and the hollyhocks,
but still each night I mend your cotton socks.
Now our little boy has the chicken pox.
Ulysses, honey, when you coming home?

The men hanging round are just boys to me.
One from Trinidad. One from Tallahassee.
But I need more than boys to stir my sugar tea.
Ulysses, honey, when you coming home?

All night I'm waiting by the telephone.
I haven't paid the bill and I'm all alone.
Don't you ever hear those voices in the dial tone?
Ulysses, honey, when you coming home?

Life without you is a heart attack.
You just got your suitcase and started to pack.
I know you'll come driving a brand-new Cadillac.
Ulysses, honey, when you coming home?

You're a man who couldn't cross the ocean
without making a scene or some sort of commotion.
Out in the sun you'd forget your suntan lotion.
Ulysses, honey, when you coming home?

I'm tired of living on government checks.
They buy the Jack Daniel's. They're no good for sex.
Now they tell me you left no forwarding address.
Ulysses, honey, when you coming home?

Last night I had the strangest vision.
Two big bay horses had a collision,
and there was your face on the television.
Ulysses, honey, when you coming home?

GRAY'S ANATOMY

O doctor, dear doctor, my husband,
he calls them the rudest names.
He calls mine Annie Oakley.
He calls his Jesse James.

I love to squeeze his Cutty Sark
as he rounds my Cape of Good Hope,
but why must he leak his fountain pen
in my business envelope?

And why are these Egg McMuffins,
and why is that steak tartare?
And why does he say my rack of lamb
has the smell of caviar?

He loves to lift my Dixie cups.
He leaves my bacon charred.
He drives my little rental car
by inserting his MasterCard.

He wants to put his dessert spoon
into my raspberry fool
or take his New York minute
inside my Liverpool,

or put his plug in my outlet,
his sirloin in my roaster,
his dreadnought up my river mouth,
his toolbox in my toaster.

Whenever we're in the bedroom,
he whispers in my ear
that I'm his drowning Ophelia
and he's my young King Lear.

And then he strips me naked
to kiss my razor clam
or puts his thumb like a diplomat
deep into Vietnam.

SMALL BAD TOWN

The fractional white moons
of the satellite dishes
bother the broken noons
and the mortal wishes

of the local housewife
burning from her soaps.
Time sends invitations
in little envelopes.

The Spanish moss like hunger
hangs from the dogwood tree,
and no one pays the phone bill
of eternity.

Worship the devil of plenty,
worship the devil of wrath,
whose lovesick Brahma thunders
up the garden path.

O Protestant God, forgive us,
you Age of Steam antique.
The river floods its banks
and the flesh is weak.

Look! An egret launches
high above the oak,
like a Pershing missile.
The cows drink Diet Coke.

Too near, white churches tower,
like chalk cliffs of Dover.
In our small bad town
the cold war's never over.

❧ 2 ☙

MILTON'S TONGUE

NOTHING

Below us the gray fields of England
lie like sacks of cement
as I fill out the landing card
of Her Majesty's government.

A girl adrift under her Walkman
is sipping her father's vin blanc.
I turn to study the orange juice
and a new moon of stale croissant,

our "continental" breakfast.
I've paid with a handful of dimes
for the vodka spilled at my feet
on the crumpled *New York Times*.

A pale silver wrinkling, or kneading,
on the green Naugahyde of sea
disturbs the aluminum cowl
of the engine by GE,

and a coarse white whisker of ship
blinks in simple Morse code
the danger of scotch on the rocks
or ice on wet strings of road

across the stubble of Dartmoor
where black pools on western slopes
surround broken needles of light
that might be needles of hope.

We are tired, bloodless figures,
the waxworks of Madame Tussaud.
How little we really expect.
How less than little we know.

The bowmen who nocked their arrows
on the fields of Agincourt
protected these gas storage tanks,
the docks of this tiny port,

the small rural railway station,
the zipper of British Rail,
the consolation of life
built on HO scale,

the silver sigh of a river
squeezed from a tube of paint,
the chalky scar of high street
and a crossing that stares like a saint.

I remember your dying, your anger,
alone in a hospital bed.
The dead help no one living
and the living no one dead.

In minutes we will be landing
at the airport of status quo. ·
We never escape very far
from the deaths that await us below.

THE LATE PERPENDICULAR OF ENGLAND

The ancient churches,
hollow with embroidered cushions and flower funds,
still smell of the other world,
the world of damp masonry and decay.

The whitewashed plaster,
once swirling with the devil of polychrome,
powders the heads of German students
light-headed from lager.

Summer filters through the grayish-blue light,
distant and calm, with that dismay,
neither human nor wholly inhuman,
of Canaletto's lost Venetian light

staining the palaces of Westminster.
Lost to the musky shades of greengages,
the ruptured Thames
was flecked with dozens of little gondolas,

dark smoked curls of Darjeeling.
When August's molten silver
sealed the mouths of saints
whose fever peeled the paint from postcard racks,

they bathed in the cold serenity of suffering.
They serve our less-than-scientific observations,
deaths abraded from slate slabs,
antique lives we have no common language with,

unless they too were lies.

THE ENGLISH LIGHT

Above the slate roofs, Turner's blinding light,
the light of the atom bomb,
glowed like a car cigarette lighter.

The center was everywhere
and circumference nowhere, like a medieval god—
his triumphal heavens reduced to X rays.

Two trees soldiered up the hill,
souls of the damned—pitiless, self-assured.
Scars of red poppies

ordered a field of minuscule, deckled cattle.
That night we set sail
on the tides of the back garden,

tire ruts burning like St. Elmo.
Something made its way through the mist—
an electric pylon with murder on its minds.

A third presence was always with us.
Our voices steamed the air
like the gossip of cattle.

Cambridge Hours

i. Leavis Before Christ's

There Leavis brooded on his Cambridge spires,
criticism's last muezzin, dreaming skylights
through the painted damp of Anglian winter.
Too short to be damned, our lives still long for souls.
The college carves lead coffins from its lawn
and cannot shift the Anglo-Saxon bones—
they rattle through the combination rooms.
The shelves are stocked in all the town museums.
His souls condensing on the freezing glass,
God drags the bass drum of His consciences
through stained-glass windows in the college walls.
Next year His students will be Japanese.
The snowbound eddies kowtow in the street,
and in our rooms, lost packaging of things to eat.

ii. Reading the Greek Gospels

Deckled by pastry chefs, our weather's French—
the street lamps bore their conscience through the frost,
a dust or powdered sugar on the slate.
The lone bell's censer whistles up the wind:
snow speaks against the glass like a hungry ghost.
Raw Christians call the parish to account
for bearish interest in the judgment day.
The church's crossbeams buckle like oak spars:
each quarter it falls further into debt.
Joan of Arc's our winter figurehead,
her lungs like flour sacks, her head a grape
oozing the smoke metaphysics calls the soul.
Inside, we wince before the room's gas fire.
The neighbor cats walk snarling through the mire.

The Old College

Long the regulation, short the money-changing
within the walls of the river college.
We walked among the gathering dusks,

gathering something beyond the ghost of ourselves.
The walnut tree had replaced the walnut tree,
the plaster of a revising century

been stripped to half-timbered hall.
Under a tower where Erasmus had scratched
a few documents in the gall of ink,

we walked the line of old cloister:
never a better view than one partially impeded.
Beyond the river, beyond the mathematical bridge,

the creaking rank of plane trees wavered,
their leaves on fire now, the fires drifting to ground.
Back, back, everything must be scraped back,

back to the monastery wall beyond the stubbled lawn,
back to the tarnished moon dial,
back to the cobbled street, the medieval thoroughfare.

We were late, too late for our appointments.
In the old hall, gaudy with painted ghosts,
a sparrow pecked the false medieval tiles.

BRIEF LIVES

i. Larkin

Hull was a rainy country. The damp of suits
slumped on their wooden hangers understairs,
the wet umbrellas dying in the hall.
The ink-stained carpet. The sodden shoes. The hats.
Beneath the street, drains took away the filth.
His head felt like a boiled egg with spectacles.
Each window streaked with rain or after-rain,
the river swollen to the mud-thick roads,
gave nothing back. One might as well get on with it.
And in the country, the drowning of the toads.

No one can imagine how the end will go,
lonely companions: the bottle and the lamp,
the naked girls who pose for you alone.
And somewhere distant, the ringing of the phone.

ii. Kant

Climbing the ladder of immortal law,
he looked down, staggered by the awful smell.
There were no safety nets above the ground.
The drop was clear into the mouth of hell.
No one could advise him. His hands were raw
from years of climbing toward a distant cloud.
He heard the angry roaring of a crowd
and felt the brush of feathers at his ear.
There was no premonition in the sound.

The crows had talked to him. They knew the worst
of sinners never die of heat or thirst,
but of not knowing why they live in fear.
Knowing the worst would never make it so.
He took one look above and then let go.

iii. Auden at C_____ C_____

The ink of twilight stains the Gothic mullions.

Before the common room's split paneling,
you mumbled to a pair of carpet slippers
the words that once had made a difference.

Old master, face graven like the ruined tracks
of Weimar Berlin, the subway lines gauged east
through stations blooming like the cereus,
how illustrate the night of Marxist doctrine,
the vague incitement to the candled mass,
now lawyers at Wall Street's famous victory?
Not one still worships at your bedded grave,

not one the gorging literary worm

whose grinning rage expels in harmless drudgery
the ink and woodpulp of the mastered will.

iv. Marx

Lacking a proper mother, he bought his lust
among the politicians and the frauds,
the old proportion of the biblical list
that guarantees to every saint a Ford.

The mocking of the press did not deter
the hollow faces calling from the mirror
in language that was blessèd like a scar
to warn him of the close of Happy Hour.

That foul night of the soul, an angry horn
woke ferrets in the steppe grass, where the finch
had bribed the tsar's officials to abandon
the blue-plate special and martini lunch.

Next morning came to eastern parliaments
too late to make alternative arrangements.

LIVING

A strip of ocher binds the distant oaks
behind the ancient professor
wrapped in a deck chair,
his hair aflame,

tongue lolling in its socket.
Spring tends its rotten corporations,
the musky horns of fluted daffodils
tilting from a vase by your hospital bed.

I lost my way to your room
and knocked at one, then another,
the old, oceanic nightmare,
behind each door the drowned husk of a face.

Outside your window a vain forsythia
fizzed with bloom
as you counted out your age:
87 now, no, 86, no 87 . . .

They wheeled you away to the porcelain baths,
the sarcophagi, you announced, of the damned Phoenicians,
and then they called you *Professore*—
like most annunciations, in a minor key.

Save us from, save all of us from hell.

PARADISE

A stunted broom plant blurs its fiery blossom
against the rotting gate,
the lumber now the color of nylon stockings—

like a rotting Creation—
and worn, too,
the grasses feel the pinch of moss,

the night's republic of the snail,
whose ragged silver ribbands sail
against the charred portion of the moon.

The British goddess lies beneath the shed
in a frieze of worm—not a Paradise,
still less what Paradise would become:

weedy, mean, trivial,
the flint knapping up through winter ground.
In the bleakest marches,

Romans never passed a night
without a pitched camp of rampart and ditch.
Your house still overlooks a prospect

of benevolent brick facades,
each concealing its private signature of garden.
Not much changes. Not much in us changes

here, beyond the material end of Paradise.

Adam and Eve

The angels stood embarrassed
in their nakedness
as if the body were a marriage of evil.
We passed beneath their lidless gaze,

entering the chapel,
into the freezing starlight
of a moon's cracked panes,
salt-edged and merciless.

We sat beneath a musty painting
where something like a deer
breasted a varnished slope.
Through brackish clouds lightning

flared, though one searing bolt
was only a rough tear in the canvas.
O sacred clumsy animal!
Out in the dusty blindness of Rome,

the ocher was peeling
from shuttered buildings in arched squares.
Starved rivulets shook in the gutters,
their oily ribbons

falling—like miniature rainbows—
into the ancient storm sewers,
and the slight, shy angle of a street
turned a distant corner, a mockery of despair.

PARADISE LOST

i. The Cities of the Plain

Reduced to skeletons, the cows
cropped the leafless, broken boughs.

As she passed, a crooked frond
muzzled the shallows of a pond.

The arbors hung with rotting grape.
Beneath them lay a sickened ape.

The full moon, torn like an evening gown,
shone its justice on the town.

From the hills, she felt a shiver
as a ferry crossed the river.

On the plain, a cone of fire
tangled up, behind barbed wire.

She realized it was no one's fault.
Now in her mouth the taste of salt.

ii. San Giorgio dei Greci

I gave to Hope a watch of mine: but he
An anchor gave to me.
　　　　　　　—George Herbert

The wrecked Ark anchored in the green lagoon,
Mount Ararat a crumbling gilt palazzo.
How could the refugees of Byzantium
embrace, in the Fall, the city that betrayed them?

Lighting the tapers of their watery faith,
the faithful gathered in the salvaged hull.
They raised a rusty anchor overhead.
The barnacled keel became the roof above them.

The dusty icons, hung like WANTED posters,
stared at the sinners like a wall of sins:
each gloomy Christ was silent to their faces
but spoke in secret to the guilt within.
Despite the sins, no man could do without them.
In the gloom, Christs gathered the gold about them.

iii. The Old God

I am your God, He said, and shook His head.
A dove flew bleeding from the broken sky
that fell like mirrors on the newly dead,
whose faith in Him He could not justify.

His mother had once taught the unreal numbers
to caracole and caper on His hand.
He gave His people manna and cucumbers
to feed them till they found the promised land.

The maps were old; the X had been erased
that marked the valley of their chosen fate.
They stumbled forth. Their kings could not predict
the Bible maps would soon be real estate.
His wayward Son was nowhere near as strict
and sold them new Armani for their waists.

iv. Nativity

The sad blue figures from the north had come
across a major desert and a sea,
hungry at first, their horses giving out,
the boats struck dumb on unforgiving shores.

The city was no city of the plain.
Women and men still coupled under sheets
and spoke half-true endearments to each other.
They wondered what three kings were doing there

and what they paid the kneeling prostitutes.
Beyond the blacksmith's stood a burnt-out inn
the comet passed over like an asterisk.
They came to see, and saw they were mistaken.
They swept away disheartened, and just missed
the door that opened on a miracle.

v. On the Crucifixions

That night the army crucified the slaves
and hung their Jesus from the city gates.
The children drew his tiny face on slates.
When tourists begged direction to the graves,

the cats who once had visions could not hear
and dogs who could read Latin would not speak.
The minister spilled his faxes in the creek,
the private crawled to bed beside his spear.

In bloody fields long overthrown with rye,
young lovers read their Nietzsche by the stones.
The crocuses confuse the shards of bone.
The pig rejects the logic of its sty.
Their Caesar dreams he is a cockatoo
gabbling of the gassing of the Jew.

vi. Eden in the Dustbowl

She was her own celestial city now.
The ravens and the crows in residence
were fallen angels of the picket fence.
Behind it stood the Devil's Jersey cow.
Each dawn a cold, forbidding sun still rose.
The dishes were still there to put away,
but something different—well, she couldn't say.
Perhaps it was the closet full of clothes.
How could she know what true confession was?
Two squalling kids, a husband on the make,
and that June evening with the coral snake—
a devil is not paid for what he does.
There, there in the clearing hung the golden bough.
She stood amid the garbage with her sow.

❧ 3 ❧

THE DISORDERED EYE

BORDER SONNETS

i.

The plains of Iowa dreamed, or seemed to dream,
the prairie dogs erect above their dens,
the corn unripening by the local Gulf.
We slept through May in the landlady's single bed,
like two wives—creaky, uncomfortable as sin,
the eagerness of sin a sin itself.
Airless at dawn, at dusk a tinderbox,
your shoebox apartment shared the slanting roof.
The alley glared in moonlight's palest talc.
One night a shout—a file of naked freshmen
steamed away, white asses hot as dimes,
onward into forgetfulness. Youth, ah youth.
We slept, and woke, and slept the day away,
careless as pigeons with their broken quills.

ii.

The bay drew out, the bay drawled in again
to peeling dories gutted like horseshoe crabs.
The lighthouse on the point swung its spiked arm,
the water glowing, dead, the waves gone black.
We perched above the tide in our mock apartment
with its Pollock floor, its clanking unsteady heat.
Across the landing, Our Lady of the Rings
gave ear to every faithless gay in P'town.
Come fall, like scallops, the wary shops clamped shut,
leaving the candlepin lanes, the A & P—
even the Portuguese bakery locked its doors.
Those winter dawns, I searched the low-tide midden
for heads of bisque dolls, fishwives white as frost.
Our neighbor had survived the Holocaust.

Those heavy, drowned-washrag, still moonless nights
our hands would test the blindness of our faces,
tourists scratching their names on marble columns
valued for the old Ionic pallor.
Ah travelers, your unmarked passports held
down for the inky stamp and the waved hand.
Where had we been, what hopes had we abandoned?
That was the summer when you couldn't sleep,
naked each night—your breasts aglow at dawn,
your clammy skin would glisten on the sheets.
The neighbors' mournful country-western songs
echoed across the lawn at three A.M.
to anything awake to mate, to breed,
to summer insects with a geisha's feet.

iv.

Silence, raw silence, the silence of despair—
how many species would Erasmus have counted,
humbling himself to his raggle-taggle couplets?
All night the driveling rain had dripped like plasma.
Our bodies lay like pickets on the bed,
sheets gaudy with the Roman red or blue.
The hardened plaster of those naked lives
chiseled from the tufa, the privacy
of death or agony all aftermath.
We stumbled the long ramp to the buried city,
the ramp to hell, the dry and dead inferno
where rich men breathed in a servant's last embrace.
The couches squatted like a Macy's display,
charged on credit, wrapped in plastic sheets.

v.

The heat. The naked heat. And then the night.
The painted bugs carved arches through the lights,
moths of the burning prairie, moths of the moon.
Who were we not to pay for our desires?
The fire sirens wheedled out their song;
the cotton-wool deafness burned my inner ear
into black Odysseys of vertigo.
Deep in the house your Singer sang its dirge.
Where were its lessons, its eerie rapt temptations,
for mouths so thin-lipped, corrupt, and curious?
The Greeks would have recognized our soiled heat,
the bruises of the mounting thunderheads.
A rough parenthesis. And then the rain—
the corrugated tin erupted like sin.

vi.

The fallen pastures under slash pine raged
as still as revelation; and blindly marched
the lumbering night slugs, their crippled progress
beneath the waving horns of the landlord snail.
The houseless cannot live to envy the housed.
Our north walls mossed in the sweet-gum's shadow.
The cabbage palms fanned upward to the sun,
life unto life, as if the soul would agree.
The tree frogs trimmed their voices to the oak's
lost garden strangled on the blackened husks.
Our tin roof, shining through each new-moon blackout,
lit up the rain-charred zones, the attic breathing
of heart pine over dry beam. A flaring match
would choke even our fallen world with ash.

Our dinner cooled, glare-ice of grease under meat;
the butter slumped, the table reeked of Ajax,
killer hero reduced to kitchen chores—
god of the stinking sink, the underworld,
moved to doubt, then moved again to anger.
Your smile, mysterious as a writhing snake,
not from Vermeer or Caravaggio,
was a painter's smear, keen-edged, approximate.
At last we've reached our ripely gutted forties.
Your breasts lay cooling through your summer shift,
deep V of sweat wicking through the cotton.
Outside the summer faltered in its own heat.
A dead raccoon curled on the back step,
its pink mouth open in a luxurious yawn.

BAD DREAM

The room was airless and damp,
the sheets a skin of sweat.
The greasy feather pillow
curled like a postage stamp.

There had been the usual violence.
On the gray Formica table,
a man in a toupee
gestured and grinned in silence

on the network evening news.
His eyes were pink as a rabbit's.
Behind him the evening sky
discolored like a bruise.

The signs lit up for bingo.
Along the dusty roadside
a shattered NO VACANCY flared
under a neon flamingo.

An ancient B-17,
red as a tin of tobacco,
lumbered down the runway
reeking of kerosene.

It rose in hope and joy
over cornfields in smoke and flame,
but as it banked an engine
dropped like a Tinkertoy.

Our kyrie eleison.
Two mushroom clouds,
sad and white as milk,
boiled over the horizon.

THE SHOCK OF THE NEW

At six o'clock, before the article of dawn begins,
rising to the housetops like a low-wattage lamp,
a weak chittering deepens in the yard.

We were not prepared for the raw sense of things,
timetables of the canal boat, the drowning cell,
the method of a madness long arranged.

By morning we have molted our evening clothes
and returned to the responsibilities of daylight,
though never the same light cast on moral geography,

the last faltering colonies and their flies.
And down in the auction room, flayed for sale,
the furniture of a criticism, religion's chesterfield,

philosophy's three-legged chair, like a crippled dog,
and the scratched side table of an elegant phrase.
The French polishers are polishing their knives.

Women are preparing to mount the carriage steps,
gathering their skirts, but not a part of history,
as history is not a part of anything else.

Not a necessary part of the derelict design.

After Horace

i. Beauty

No longer do your storm windows rattle
to the gravel of boys in Armani suits:
they're proof no longer against the slumber
    of Valium in warm milk.

The deadbolt no longer slips its mortise,
the door whisper on its hinges. You never hear,
"I've been dying for you all night long,
    baby, sweet baby."

You'll weep your turn, shriveled on 42nd Street,
no message on your answering machine,
while under moon-clouds a sulphurous wind
    whips off the East River,

and all the agèd love or pale desire
that couples the borzois on Park Avenue
will burn your ulcerated body.
    Then, then you'll be sorry

the Wall Street brokers in gold-rimmed specs prefer
their mint-green fifties to your lingerie.
They spin the crumpled leaf of your address
    into the basket.

                      (Book 1, Ode 25)

ii. Luxury

Soon the lily-white suburbs will leave nothing
for the plough, swimming pools will flood
        oceans of grain, and ancient oaks
           fall for the Oaks Mall.

Then birds of paradise and lavender roses
will perfume manicured beds of mulch
        where a farmer once harvested
           a few acres of apples.

Then we'll have Briarwood
where a thicket stood. Under Washington
        or Jefferson the tattered flag
           meant liberty or life.

They were content with slave plantations;
the great ideal was common government.
        No private citizen built a Taj Mahal
           on the shores of New Jersey;

no law allowed the rich to clear-cut native forest.
Like the steel baron Carnegie, they should
        have built libraries, or wasted marble
           on something to believe in, like God.

(Book 2, Ode 15)

THE LESSER DEPTHS

The fogbound freighter rules the uneven swell
somewhere, out there, where we are not invited.
All night the breakers unroll like bolts of wool
in fever's shell, the sleep of the uninvited.

That could be our nature, the only life
scarred, overripe, the tempting compromise
young lovers make between the shoreline's *if*
and ocean's *as* of interrupted lies,

a dreaming angelfish on a diet of dust
behind a narrow plate of mossy glass,
bloated, familiar incandescent ghost
sighting a world its Christ eyes cannot bless.

There is, I know, another sort of hell.
I feel beneath my hands the ancient chill,
weightless, unloving, as if the dead could smell
in my reflected face the scent of evil.

The Woods at M _____

Deep in the wood each dawn I heard
the shrouded question of the wren.
You wouldn't ask that question now.
        I could not answer, then.

I stood beneath two cottonwoods
whose dry leaves clacked in a pearly luster.
A throttled cry rolled out of the brush
        attached to a feather duster.

It spun and cartwheeled in the dirt,
advanced, retreated whimpering,
cocked its head, then crawled along
        dragging a crippled wing.

The woods were half on fire with drought
that late July, when I had strayed.
You loved me then with all the passion
        of someone first betrayed.

For a Woman in United Germany

What do the birds believe in, in Stuttgart?
I can see them, oily rags
around the fountains in the central square.
Are there fountains? Is there a square?

There are miniature mountains,
because you describe them,
and suburbs draped over them
like dirty canvases. Are the suburbs relaxing,

or just tired, tired of winter?
On our boarded-up shops,
a black girl stood naked to the waist,
young breasts cupped in a man's chalky hands.

Soon white strips
covered her body like shreds of clothing
and she'd been torn a new mouth.
I think of yours, voted into pure verb.

Is there snow on the traitors now?
The moss-green slopes you crossed,
shiny and deceptive as lingerie—
where are the lies buried now?

The ramshackle sheds tilt north and south;
the barbed-wire posts and broken bushes
crook fingerlike out of the ground.
They kept their language and they lost their lives.

Song

Her nose is like a satellite,
her face a map of France,
her eyebrows like the Pyrenees
crossed by an ambulance.

Her shoulders are like mussel shells,
her breasts nouvelle cuisine,
but underneath her dress she moves
her ass like a stretch limousine.

Her heart is like a cordless phone,
her mouth a microwave,
her voice is like a coat of paint
on a sign by Burma-Shave.

Her feet are like the income tax,
her legs a fire escape,
her eyes are like a video game,
her breath like videotape.

True love is like a physics test
or a novel by Nabokov.
My love is like ward politics
or drinks by Molotov.

FOR THE HOSTAGES

They wanted to sell wheat, spare parts, and weapons.
The Secretary minded his own business.
In Tokyo, he received a cable.
The Colonel's secretary had transposed two words.

It was unseemly to ask a foreign government for money.
The President would be gravely damaged.
The Secretary had deliberately been left in the dark.
If there was a villain, it was the Admiral.

The Secretary had a hazy idea what the real story was.
The men around the President considered him an enemy.
The President was prone to delusions of grandeur.
The Colonel's secretary had transposed two numbers.

The Admiral's days were numbered.
Numbers often reveal more than they intend.
The President sent an unmistakable message.
If there was a spare part, it was the Admiral.

The money was deposited in the wrong account.
In no version is there any hint of an altercation.
The President had not made up the numbers.
The Colonel's secretary had transposed two enemies.

Not until months later was the wheat recovered.
Now the President's wife went into action.
She wanted to end this matter once and for all.
If there was a wrong account, it was the Admiral's.

Not until months later had the press recovered.
The President blamed them for questioning his numbers.
He had learned numbers and forgotten numbers.
The President had made up his mind.

The weapons did not come without problems.
The spare parts did not come without an enemy.
The wheat did not come without delusions.
The sources did not come without weapons.

The Livery of Byzantium

Now prisms of the damp, disordered eye
betray the eastern border where the lamb
throws down its milk, the banded owl calls down

dominion on the pathways of the mouse.
More light! More light! The meager shaft of grace,
no brazen ore through its hot galleries,

conceals the daily forgeries of spring.
There, beyond the weevil and the worm
gavotting on the corpses of fresh kill,

a sun-blown apple tree, its trunk black pitch,
its petals wrought from white-hot iron bars,
opens to the sweet rank of corruption.

In all religion comes the purchase of
a scrap of cloth, the holy wounds that buy
the almost living and securely dead.

And death awaits the tender flock of sheep.

THE WORDS

He wrote the words then; they would have to do.
He hadn't known the words had been forbidden,
or that in other hands they were not new.
He couldn't see just what in them was hidden,

or why his fathers had been paid to speak
a language whose intentions all were planned.
The withered storks who cried in ancient Greek
would never know their meanings had been banned.

The cunning of his verbs was not mistaken,
the gaze of his dry adjectives not flawed.
But when he tried to show just what he'd meant,

they claimed his meanings were an accident,
and every guilty subtlety a fraud.
The words once put to sleep would not awaken.

⚜ 4 ⚜

THE DARK REALM

ELEGY

When they die young, we have no right to mourn
the loss. We suffer losses every day.
I saw your ghost amid the alien corn.

Standing there, deaf to us all, it seemed to scorn
the racket of the mockingbird and jay.
When they die young, we have no right to mourn.

How could your mothballed wedding dress adorn
the rose-decked coffin like a virgin May?
I saw your ghost. Amid the alien corn,

it crossed the broken fields. The old moon's horn
hung over the prayers—I had no words to pray.
When they die young, we have no right to mourn

the lives they would have led, the pages torn
across the calendar of dates unfinished. Stay—
I saw your ghost amid the alien corn.

How much it cost, that terrible beauty born
amid the ruin of our cold clichés.
When they die young, we have no right to mourn.
I saw your ghost amid the alien corn.

for Tamela James (1967–1994)

DEAR JM

There in the shallows, you were treading water,
still a boy of twenty though a man of sixty,
your shock of gray hair burning white

as if immersed in bleach. The day grew hotter.
In this world, the other world is more distant,
your broken willowware teacup

rocking on a hook in someone's kitchen,
far from your homemade Ouija board.
No mirrors show you've left behind

your aging friends, no longer boys themselves.
Your house in Stonington is a closed tomb
where ghosts like midges come clotting the evening.

When Odysseus knelt before the blood-filled pit,
the ghosts streamed out, anxious for news,
one after the other, pleading, pleading . . .

Only one lingered, one who could not
walk forward to taste the blood, giant Ajax
who stepped back into the dark without a word.

The postman stands on our porch
in pith helmet and bush shorts,
sweating in subtropical heat,

but he brings no postcards from you.

for James Merrill (1926–1995)

Dear AC

I lifted the tea tray over the slanting lawn
in Grantchester's withered apple orchard,
crusts of your sandwich gathering

a mock empire of ants, black ships swanning
the uncharted distance to Japan.
Cambridge was a closed city,

its gardens unkempt pathworks (I mean *patchworks*)
of ivy behind high walls. Here and there
a rotted gate, a broken slatted door,

gave onto a view of the ordered life.
The vision of roses, the philosophical
dented watering can, even the laboring bees,

not Marx's but Bentham's,
took their liberties within their lies.
I could never be religious again.

What lingered in *New* England that last morning, as dawn
carried the frost off shard by shard,
away from the cardinal with the battered wing

who feathered, ghostlike, and began to sing—
or creak, really? Over your bed no feather of fan
drifted down, as if from pity,

no owl kept watch, no arguing meadowlark.
The air you breathed was not the air.
There was your red dress on the floor,

there the fruit and the greasy knife,
there your stones, your broken shells,
there your *Sonnets from the Portuguese*

(awful book). There the grieving telegrams.
What are poets without their lives?
Are they less poetic, then?

for Amy Clampitt (1920–1994)

Dear HM

Sunset. The sea is rowdy tonight,
low pines slouching toward the flats,
painted woods narrow as a lizard's back
between your boarded-up house

and that emptiness Death improves on.
Where have you gone, traveler?
To the restaurant serving clouds
of the greasy broth you took nervous,

brave delight in after your heart attack?
No, there you sit, cloudy in your deck chair
(auctioned from the derelict *Queen Mary*),
awaiting martinis on a pitted tray

from your shipshape nautical kitchen,
your "garden" more a sandbox
in which a few tarry bushes
have run aground. Lost souls.

Lost souls of lost summers,
the teak of the deck chair growing paler,
year by year, your figure more ghostly—
finally thin enough! Thin as galley proofs!

That would be your hell, no calls returned,
not even the diagramless *Times* puzzle,
just the looking forward
to the one long look back.

for Howard Moss (1922–1987)

DUNE HOUSE

The house sat
between the dunes, like driftwood,
and the owners looked like driftwood—
he had a beard like fishing line,

and she had seaweed for hair.
All day they cooked soups,
throwing in whatever the tide had hauled up—
a dogfish, a can of asparagus, pearly

baby squid, even a little beach glass.
Live off the land? They lived off the tide,
every morning down to the shore
to see what had come ashore.

They went off like clockwork (but the tide
ran backward, an hour earlier every morning).
The houses, one by one, were retiring,
slipping off their stilts in a gale,

losing their siding, absentmindedly,
or taking a big breath one morning and collapsing.
The broad Atlantic looked like a father,
stern and brooding,

inching unhappily up the shore
and leaving behind a jigsaw of shells
that couldn't be glued back together.
We had to flatten our tires to drive on the sand,

rolling along the tide mark,
the tires squashed Os.
The stormy ocean spun with froth,
like caps of cream in a mixing bowl. Gulls

coasted the beach, refusing to come down.
Suddenly one would make a batlike *screak*
and give a jump in the air.
Atop the shipwreck of a house,

a little chimney struggled to make smoke.
(Inside, the woodstove shivered to keep warm.
It couldn't keep us warm—it couldn't keep itself warm.)
The inside of the house felt like an old poem—

of course! "The End of March."
Even the Atlantic was the same,
the sky etched like beach glass,
everywhere else clear and hot.

We were ice cold.
Finally we drank up our soup. It was time to go.
We followed our old track
(otherwise we might have been stuck there forever),

and we never went back.

for Elizabeth Bishop (1911–1979)

Dear DD

The paperboy arrived, the afternoon
of your first byline
in *The Boston Evening Transcript,*
and into the yard rattled your dapper fiancé,

the Quaker Oats salesman
in his company car.
You put the paper aside. The photographs
of that other world, so near to us

in black and white.
Eighty years have put the city in the country,
the pruned gardens out of date
as whalebone corsets.

Your grandfather, a packet captain
on the North River, young captain of captains,
was salt-preserved and famous as far as Fall River.
And then *your* parents,

impossibly aged, black-worsted beetles
emerging with canes from their forties Packard.
In the attic their tilting piles of unread *Time.*
Here Bobbie and Gampie,

brand-new as cellophane, lie in your shoebox,
her tea shop and his grocery,
all that life we could wish for them,
and then wish for ourselves.

Old and then young again, old then young,
like a fairy tale. Beneath the last curling Kodaks,
William at Humarock, emperor of castles
swept by the next tide.

Or *is* it me?
As you lay on your deathbed,
plastic tubes through your nose,
your daughter my mother could not rouse you.

Your eyes had that thousand-yard stare.
"It's William," I said. "William, the poet."
Your eyes cleared and you looked at me,
and then, in a hoarse, hunted whisper,

"You   only   think   you   are."
for Dorothy Drew Damon (1900–1994)

My Father as Madame Butterfly

The dark blue stain across the river
staggers under the lightning.
The radio plays Puccini.
He turns back to the mirror with his razor,

my father, holding it like a dowsing rod.
When it comes, he will be ready—
the main chance, the ship coming in.
Happy families are all alike.

That's what they tell the other families.
Out the window, the little town is rousing,
a flock of grackles
blacking the sky like construction paper.

The boxlike milk truck chuffs up the street.
Fishing boats have hauled anchor
at Lee's Wharf. Beneath the floating dock,
rare petals of algae bloom.

There above our bunk beds, trophies,
the swords of swordfish,
blunted, bony, a curdlike gray.
The thrash and curl of battles underwater:

a Dürer woodcut on the plain of blood,
men tramped underfoot by armed horse
or pierced by lowly footman's pike.
A petal of blood

curves across my father's cheek—
he's nicked an old scar.
Was that *Superman* we were reading,
or *Man and Superman?*

for W. Donald Logan, Jr. (1925–1990)

MANHATTAN TRANSFERS

i. Inferno

Consoling, or not consoling, still
the distant oncoming first-a-squeak-
then-a-roar tympanic democracy

(from many voices one) of the IRT
assures the impatient traveler unsoothed
by the near absence of schedule, slave

to the catch-as-catch-can unpredictable
arrival, so much like the mechanical
impossible-to-brake workings of a fate

with its own underground
railway—crossing not over but beneath
the pollution-scoured habitat of the brought-

back-from-extinction ghost of the Atlantic
salmon—that sooner or undoubtedly
later Charon's screeching aluminum Budd Car

stamped F for Fate or Future, glistening
with anticipation for that narrow
dark hereafter after death, cleansed

by toxic chemical of the John
Hancock of graffiti, the soul's doomed attempt
(once by spray can or marker, now

by ice-skater's diamond flourish scarred
into Du Pont's hazy Plexiglas miracle,
carbon etching into hydrocarbon

its secret name) to warn (*mene*)
the soulless mob of travelers, the moving finger (*mene*)
predicting that such a Cassandra, at a time (*tekel*)

unanticipated, out of darkness (*upharsin*)
and heading again into darkness,
like a life all too short, will finally arrive.

ii. *Purgatorio*

Not *Bleak House* or *Moby-Dick*, *Don Quixote* or
Anna Karenina, none of the furniture
that measured the past (reading having

been a way of marking time, an escapement),
none of the fashionable but now out-of-
date Chippendale couches where fresh

anticipations declined toward the blank page
of ending—that the dead never talk about books
would not surprise the desert fathers,

for whom the word's embodied flesh
was a new currency of desire (O
that desire were confined to inky

recesses of paper, paged out of love so
periodic its syntax longs for the full stop).
Paolo and Francesca can no longer say,

Quel giorno più non vi leggemmo avante.
The dead incarnate the flesh, Freud's
dream work unavailable until the stop-

and-go of Muybridge's cameras caught
in the eye's nervous shutter the housemaid's
shudder or horse's gallop (solving in a grainy

flash that apocalyptic question, whether the horse's
hooves all left the ground at once). Having forever
infected the painter's eye, how could the future

of the past have been less than such soul-
snatching emulsions, compressed like layers of paint
or leaves of book or the dark pastry of coal,

been other than it is, replacing dream with sin?
The shades coming to Odysseus, eager for news,
want the quickened breathing of the movie screen.

iii. Paradiso

Hopper's graying haggle of brickwork,
stairway of pointed mortar jogging
up the spent orchid facade (though

austere and even prim at this unvisited-by-
garbage-truck-or-pallet-shifter hour, still never
quite mute, calling to Beaux Arts washes

in foxed, unhunted plates, each filigree
of brick entablature, rebate, short amputated
arc of lintel a vocabulary of masonic

ritual, lingua franca comprehensible
as Latin to a medieval priest in the flooded
marches of Rumania) leaps

(*l'amor*) to fresh dawn, French windows not
(*che move*) blazing or burning to the east-
(*il sole*) facing annunciation of Earth's untidy

familiar recession, but taking all in its as-
it-were wobbly stride, glinting mirrors
(*e l'altre stelle*) beneath another sterile bandage

gauzing the Manhattan sky, gun barrel
bluing that grows by the minute bluer, until
even grief has no purchase, no credit card

eager for future debt—stoic, placid,
dawn's necessary facade on this reborn
phoenix of city, now irritable with Johnny-come-

early rush-hour traffic, the protect-my-nestlings
siren of a patrol car down Houston,
the deathlike rush of others elsewhere,

never to be met or disliked for their
failure to be other than not and never you,
now that you, too, are among the missing.

for Amy Clampitt (1920–1994)

＊ 5 ＊

THE FALL OF BYZANTIUM

*The firm tower, that is Ahab; the volcano,
that is Ahab; the courageous, the undaunted,
and victorious fowl, that, too, is Ahab; all are Ahab;
and this round gold is but the image of the rounder
globe, which, like a magician's glass, to each and
every man in turn but mirrors back his own
mysterious self.*

MOBY-DICK

PERA PALAS

Up. Up. The greasy cables creaked,
raising the polished cage of mahogany
through the marble stairway to the clouds.

The clouds were Turkish, frothy, cracked,
Tiepolo's angelic hangers-on just pigeons now,
veering shadows across the skylight's filthy glass.

The grand, or grand-no-more, hotel
looked down on the steam-wreathed Golden Horn,
glazing the seven hills of ancient Istanbul.

Atop each kneeling hill a gray mosque
squatted, its narrow minarets
aimed like Pershing missiles at their god.

Each view not a lie, but the fossil of a lie,
the windows flickering at dusk, recessed ministries
to the low chime, the wing-collared visitors

slung in sedan chairs past gathered boats,
like diplomats nestled for concession,
past the steaming locomotive and the nut seller.

We inherit but never inhabit the past,
blistered pieties betrayed by a word,
winched in the *deus ex machina* to bespattered heaven.

SPICE BAZAAR

The honey dripped from comb,
dripped from pastry in dusty glass cases,
dripped from the tomb. In the Spice Bazaar,

men swarmed around us (*the street of men*,
you called it), offering whatever might be desired,
whatever could be sold. Outside, men beckoned

behind their brass shoeshine boxes. Boxes?
Damascened brass houses like upside-down pyramids,
lost Babels of the shoe, ruined empires of the sole,

mosques of the strange inverted god.
To approach his trays of glass bottles
with brass minaret caps, you had to take off your shoes,

or felt you had to. The tongue was strange.
The tongue was English, deep in the bazaar,
each shop its domed bay, the wares calling, calling:

split chests of Ceylon, mountains of powdery spices
like truncated towers of paint—the dull, rubbed greens
of henna, brown desert of cinnamon,

scorched turmeric, each pleasure crumbled to dust.
Holbein might summon a handful of crushed lapis
for blue, a pinch of ground pearl for pearl. Anything

that might exist, could be yours for millions of lira—
all you had to do was spend it. The tunnel of shops
opened a land without forgiveness.

When the devil comes, he comes bearing gold chains
and beads of frankincense and myrrh, saying,
If you want to spend your money, I can help you.

GALATA TOWER

By the wrong streets, in the wrong quarter,
street of electrical gizmos, street of ugly lamps,
we looked for the spiky remnant of lost Genoese,

rearing like a chess rook above the Golden Horn.
The cloud-topped former Tower of Christ
rose two hundred feet, slick as a hose—

the elevator boy was tinier, more worn than his uniform,
the top floor now an all-night nightclub
(or NITE KLUP, as signs elsewhere had it).

You thought you heard the jazzy clamor of a horn—
alas, only the tinned buzz of the muezzin,
religion slipping across shattered tiles.

Here Jews were welcomed in, the Moors,
the Greeks and Anatolians, and later the embassies.
Each rejected people found its home and built walls,

and the walls burned. Behind you Asia gleamed,
white ferries plied the currents of the Bosphorus,
where glittering dolphins leapt toward the Black Sea.

Behind you a tower of bread chunks spiraled like bricks
into the Tower of Babel. *There it is!* you said.
There's the tower we've been looking for!

HAGHIA SOPHIA

Mute before the example of the gods,
even the cold stone has ambitions for itself.
In some heresies the damned are not damned,

but live on through the rusting mist of the past,
neither sinning nor failing to sin.
The haggard churches adapt to new religion,

cool mosaics flayed from the walls like skin,
a few gold emperors dumbly staring.
The light falls inward, inward, on the scaffolding.

Like river flukes, visitors carry their blindness,
fingering through Egypt's porphyry,
the starched white linen of Marmara rock,

shattered greens of Thessaly's *verde antico*.
The Christian God took His powers from the sand
and left His powers to sand again: a thousand years

bequeathed stray chisel marks, cold plots of betrayal,
fires pitched against the living wall, the broken gate,
gold tesserae reduced to a palmful of dice.

ALEXANDER SARCOPHAGUS

Heaven, like most heavens, was built for followers,
not the iconoclast or stiff-necked heretic
but the time-serving, kowtowing companion to gods.

The killer dawns that Alexander faced,
each horizon fresh-stocked with enemies,
left smoking cities behind, steaming litter of corpses,

a backwash of retired sergeants made king.
The past doddered in the dark like a sculptor's mallet,
rose in the royal necropolis, where the last kings of Sidon

were consigned to flesh-eating stone.
The stone had a life before it devoured a life,
before worked into rims of egg and tongue,

drilled scroll of grapevine, the doll-like figures at hunt:
now the panther learning the edge of the axe,
now a Persian kneeling—then a knife in the neck.

The bloodtide washed across the steppes
until the moon of Alexander was stopped by a virus,
red lance frozen to his scarred hand. The stone

turned naked stone again, even the good laid to rest
where the past has no need for forgiveness
and the future no need to pardon.

GREAT PALACE

Ambition was a word used of the losers;
the conqueror called his itches destiny.
Mosaics had been laid like documents,

ragged, stained at the edges, holed like cloth,
like fragments scrabbled from a Jerusalem *genizeh,*
saved against ruin if they named their god.

The mosaics had been continents,
terra incognita on stone intemperate seas:
there the elephant strangled a mangy lion with its trunk;

there the gods who crossed this colonnaded walk
left nothing of their scrawled affairs of state
but footprints on the portraits of delirium.

Art never questions its before, or answers its after:
there two boys rode a gallumphing camel;
there the warrior exited, followed by bear;

there the exhausted wolf gnawed the thigh of its prey.
A century later an emperor changed his mind
and silenced the old sea with marble flagstone.

BASILICA CISTERN

From the Belgrade Forest to Justinian, the iced,
mountain-bled waters, stolen by rough streams,
fed this black forest of columns

melting in slow humid vapors,
the marble skins tattooed in copper stains
like grief-green valleys, the walls moist as a mouth.

What survives is not love but order,
the remnants of a past refused by the past,
slag heap of disused temples—

pierced Corinthian under herringbone brick,
one plain shaft chased in peacock feathers,
and the giant severed heads of placid Medusae,

knowing in banishment as the head of John the Baptist.
One lolls on its side. Half-immersed, they sleep
in unflinching greens, blank eyes staring greedily

at the Victorian tourist rowed past,
lanterns held toward brick domes
flickering above, the old religion drowned below.

In the few living inches of water, motley carp
twist in supplication and arousal.
We came to see the past, but the past was blind.

Aqueduct of Valens

The Muslim moon, moon of the tropics,
curves into the reverse arch of Valens' aqueduct,
rising in slow motion, back, back from the seven hills,

fallen to ruin in the Gypsy quarter,
to ruin where the Kalenderhane Camii—
mosque of dervishes, church of the Theotokos—

shoulders its pierced wall, quarters
where every third house has burst its clapboards,
unpainted wood scorched to lifelessness.

No one survives the pastness of the past,
though Byzantine villages chose—unconditional
surrender at swordpoint or three days of pillage,

the church forfeit to an alien god.
For days the aqueduct ran a Bosphorus of blood,
the city lost in a thousand years of beauty sleep.

Think of each poison scattered over the grave,
not the salt of vengeance on vengeance,
but poisons that bring electric life again:

Ahab and his Leyden jar, charging his mates' harpoons—
Short draughts—long swallows, men; 'tis hot as Satan's hoof—
mystical white city run to ground at last.

CHURCH OF CHRIST PANTOCRATOR

Beyond the dust of the avenue, the dust of age,
mounds of dust, acres of dust, dust of dust,
like the vision of dust in *Our Mutual Friend,*

the lopsided brick church knelt above the ruckus,
nestled in ramshackle wooden houses, ruin of ruins
where women argued the peddler out of used clothing.

We climbed the slow license of the hill,
the cobbles crosshatched as an embattled etching.
Christ the Almighty, Christ the Pantocrator,

the triple church of the triple God,
God of our dumbstruck childhoods. That dusk,
by the Aqueduct of Valens, you met your childhood,

Turkish girl who rewarded you with quick hugs
and the brush of a kiss, then vanished, leader of the pack.
I remember, I was once Queen of the Backyards.

The church pitched ever beyond us, like first love
before we know what we were isn't what we are.
The past was closed to us. The past was closed for restoration.

Theodosian Walls

Cowering before Achilles and his bronze-breasted Greeks,
Troy's sacred towers are not so sacred now,
ground down to the mud of Hissarlik.

The walls of Byzantium stand more or less intact,
decorous yellow masonry decorated
with courses of red brick, like the veins of Vesalius.

Four stooping towers are inherited by a fifth
with a gaudy appendix scar, a sixth toppled on itself,
another with a brooding vaginal interior

where a peasant farmer scratches out dusty crops
on the plain between inner and outer wall.
The towers juddered down the withered valley

of the Lycus, now a hot boulevard where Urban's cannon
reduced the walls to dust, down, down to the Golden Horn,
passing the insignificant sally port, the Kerkoporta,

shyly concealed by a tower, forgotten and left open.
The Turks were within.
The emperor stood glittering with three companions,

defending an inner gate—his cousin Theophilus,
the Spaniard Don Francisco, and John Dalmata.
Theophilus yawled for death and vanished into the Turks.

Dark as leather, already chiseled like a mosaic,
the emperor removed his insignia and shouldered into battle.
Then he became dust, and less than dust.

The Fall of Byzantium

29 May 1453

Raw geometry of fourteen miles of wall.
7,000 defenders vs. 100,000 on the plain.
The Sultan's irregulars, the Bashi-bazouks,

steaming into the breaches—Hungarians, Germans,
Slavs, Greeks who had kissed the Sultan's coin.
Greek bled against Greek at the Mecca of loot.

As walls fell, beside the hungry Christians
the Ottoman pretender Prince Orhan
fought on, swearing. A day later he was beheaded.

The scarred Genoese, Giovanni Giustiniani Longo,
who beached with seven hundred veterans
and took command of the land walls. Who fought

until shot through the breastplate, begged
to be carried off by stretcher, who fired the rout.
Or Cardinal Isidore, auctioned to a genial merchant,

having bartered his gold robes for a beggar's rags.
The beggar in finery was not so fortunate.
The Sultan, twenty-seven, son of a slave girl,

his features those of a parrot about to eat cherries.
And Hasan the Giant, raw meat of the Janissaries,
scimitar ringing like a tuning fork, hacking his way

across the stockade to claim, over the split bodies of Greeks,
the Sultan's purse—*a name surviving the nameless dead*—
like Ahab taking the doubloon for Moby-Dick.

Kariye Camii

If each gold tessera holds the image of the universe,
its flaws the very galaxies, the watchful gods
stare down from their domes, weak for the sin

of profusion. The borrowed gleam of disinfected saints
lights the closed arches and filled mosaics
where the traveling philosopher might mistake

the palace of the word. In heaven, that shining city,
no language will be necessary, every suffering
inspected by the pure light that swallows all.

The martial angels guard the greasy plain
where, each devil armed with a dictionary,
the dusty battle of heaven will next be fought.

When the city fell, not glorious again
until Sinan's mosques swarmed every hill,
the primitive St. Savior in Chora,

stripped to mud-colored brick, or brick-colored mud,
survived the accidental neighborhood
where death operated its little business.

Gone, the long arrows and battered shields; gone,
corpses in their thousands, the emperor's headless body
tagged by eagled greaves and embroidered socks;

gone, the ransacked, desolate graves.
St. Luke's painting of Mary, brandished above the walls,
was hacked to pieces, torn fragments of the universe.

Here a Muslim soldier stole into the church and was amazed.

Notes

"St. John and the Wasps": Aristophanes' *The Wasps,* the plagues of Egypt, and St. John's Apocalypse.

"Song": An homage to an unpublished poem, titled "Nonsense Song," by W. H. Auden.

"For the Hostages": Some phrases are indebted to a two-part article by Theodore Draper in *The New York Review of Books:* "The Iran-Contra Secrets," May 27, 1993, and "Iran-Contra: The Mystery Solved," June 10, 1993.

ABOUT THE AUTHOR

William Logan is the author of four earlier books of poems, *Sad-faced Men* (1982), *Difficulty* (1985), *Sullen Weedy Lakes* (1988), and *Vain Empires* (1998). He has published two books of criticism, *All the Rage* (1998) and *Reputations of the Tongue* (1999). He has won the Peter I. B. Lavan Younger Poets Award from the Academy of American Poets and the Citation for Excellence in Reviewing from the National Book Critics Circle. He lives in Florida and in Cambridge, England.